"The only Pain in
Rugby is Regret"

A great figure or physique is nice, but it's self-confidence that makes someone really sexy.

STAR
104.5
In Memory of
Greg Gibbins
NSW
CUP

STAR
104.5
In Memory of
Greg Gibbins

NSW
CUP

ZIBARA
NSW CUP
NSW
In Memory of
Greg Gibbins
WYONG ROOS
EST 1910
austbrokers
central coast
insurance brokers

19

17

11

Jaycar
7
forex

Jaycar
Electronics
16

STEEDEN

THE GOOD GUYS
PLUMBING

LAKES
GLAZING
GREG MENKEN PLUMBING
STAR104.5

NSW
CUP
NSW

15

STAR104.5
austbrokers

STAR 104.5
STAR 104.5

STAR
104.5
NSW CUP
ZIBARA
In Memory of

NSW CUP

BOQ

10

STEEDEN

6
ounties
mou

VB
mounties

austbrokers
central coast
insurance brokers
POWERADE
POWERADE

THE GOOD GUYS
central coast
insurance brokers

12
15

7
POWERADE
NEWTOWN
BSC

HAWKS
4

ZIBARA
NSW CUP
NSW
In Memory of
Greg Gibbins
WYONG ROOS
EST 1910

BUNDABERG RED
BUNDABERG RED

17
Luxbet
VB

NSW CUP

FOX

SYDNEY
Roosters
ZIBARA
NSW CUP
NSW
In Memory of
Greg Gibbins
WYONG ROOS
EST 1910
central

ZIBARA
STEEDEN

ZIBARA
In Memory of
Greg Gibbins
STEEDEN

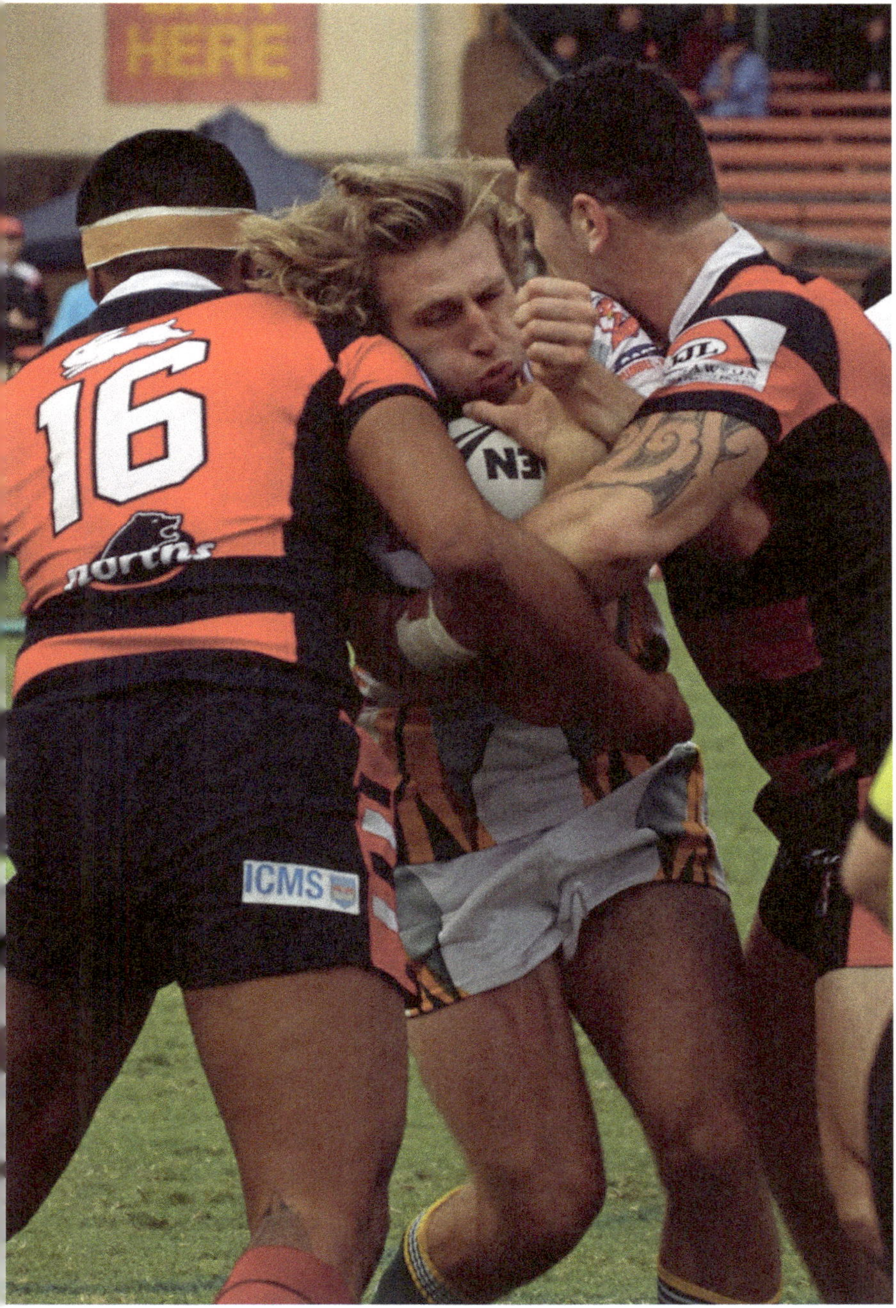
HERE
16
norths
ICMS

STEEDEN
M&J
Steggles

Jaycar
11
forex
M&J

STEEDEN

THE GOOD GUYS
TUGGERAH

11
STEEDEN
austbrokers
central coast

11
STEEDEN

STEEDEN

STAR
104.5

STAR
104.5
NSW
CUP
STEEDEN

1
norths
10
norths

SYDNEY
STAR
ZIBARA
NSW CUP
In Memory of
Greg Gibbins

NSW CUP
austbrokers
central coast
STEEDEN
GREG
MENKEN
PLUMBING
JETS

RSL
7
PETERSHAM
BOTANY VIEW
HOTEL

Insurance
moment
media

HAWKS
8

central coast

NSW
CUP
NSW
CLASSIC

NSW CUP
NSW
NSW CUP

GREG
MENKEN
PLUMBING
NRL

NSW CUP

NSW
CUP
NSW
CLASSIC
WYONG ROOS
1910

NSW CUP

GROUP SEC

austbrokers
central coast
insurance brokers

NSW CUP
central coast
insurance brokers

NSW CUP
NSW
CLASSIC
WYONG ROOS
1910

GOOD GUYS

Sense
12

NSW CUP
NSW
STAR104.5
EST 1910
austbrokers
central coas

16

16

16

10
norths
NSW CUP

9
16

CAFE2U
.com.au
15
norths

NSW

GOOD GUYS

Hisense
17
Luxbet
STEEDEN
Luxbet
8

17

austbrokers
central coast

17
Luxbet

austbrokers
central coast
insurance brokers

central coast
insurance brokers

STEED
THE GOOD GUYS

Hisense
17
14

17
Luxbet

NSW CUP
CLASSIC
EST 1910
central coast
insurance brokers

central coast
insurance brokers

8
Luxbet

Lightning Source UK Ltd.
Milton Keynes UK
UKHW020703280219
338142UK00001B/18/P

9 780368 302367